This Book Belongs To:

_____

Welcome To The
ICE CREAM
ABC ADVENTURE!

Get ready to scoop up some learning fun!

In this book, each letter of the alphabet has a delicious moment with ice cream. From A to Z, you'll discover how each letter reacts in a silly, sweet way!

Trace uppercase & lowercase letters

Draw pictures starting with that letter

Match letters and build recognition

Watch each letter transform into a fun object like an ant or an airplane.

This book helps kids build literacy skills, fine motor skills, creativity & confidence — all through play!

A Admired It

It sparkled and swirled.
So many flavors.
So Little Time.

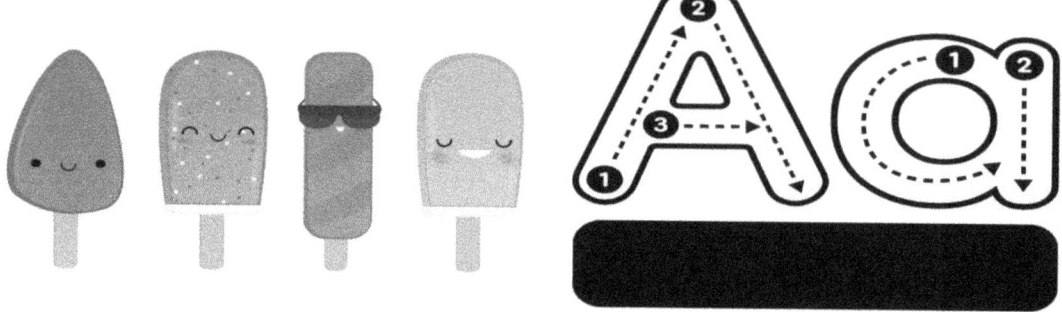

Trace the uppercase letters.

A A A A A A A
A A A A A A A

Trace the lowercase letters.

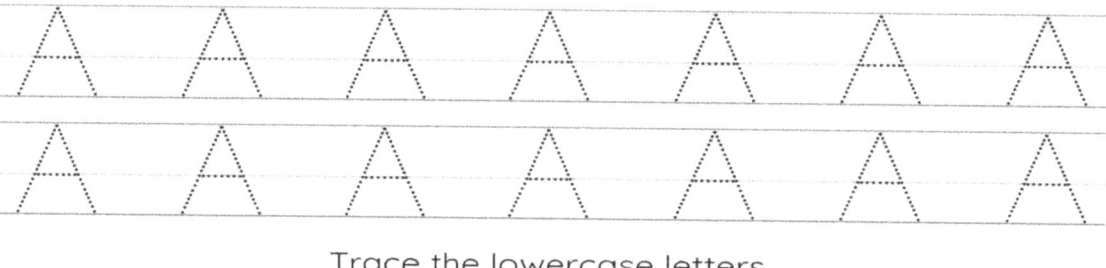

a a a a a a a
a a a a a a a

Circle the letter A & a.

B W P k J e d A z g
d t a R L O m u x
c A E e g s z K J a N

Ant

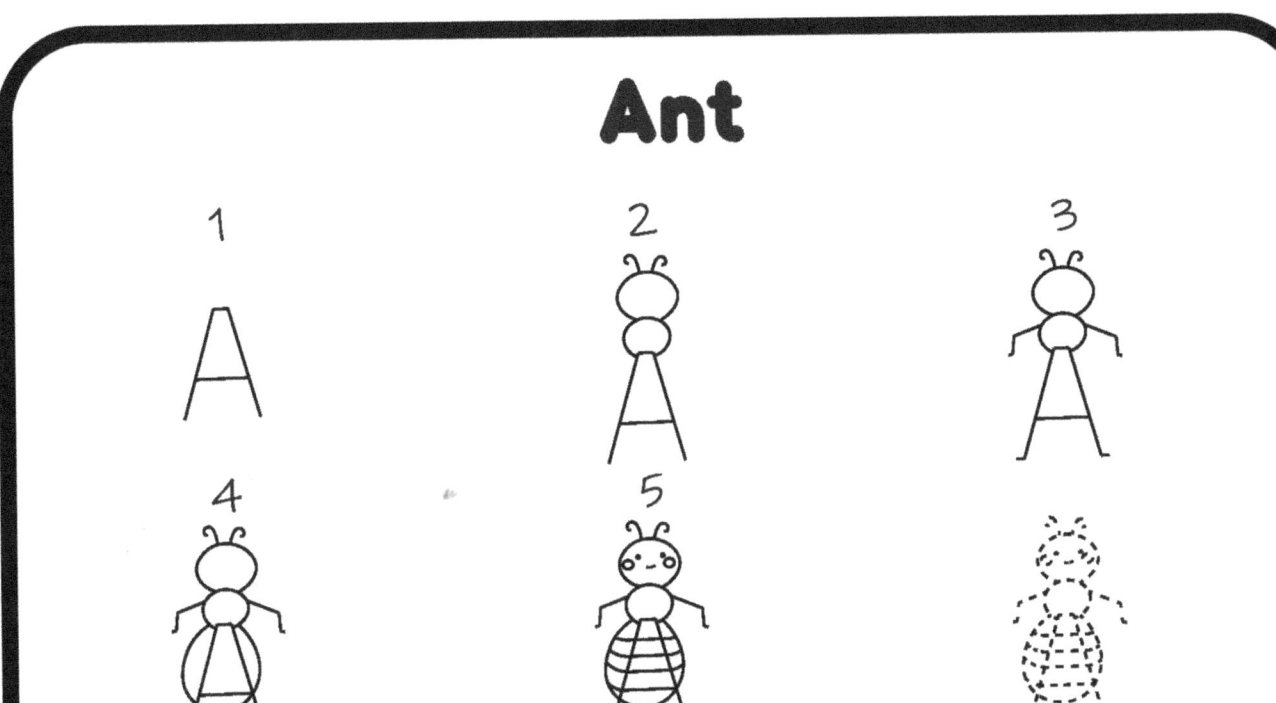

1   2   3

4   5

 Your Turn:

draw, trace, and color!

B Balanced it.

Whoa! Careful!
It wobbled and
wiggled...

Trace the uppercase letters.

B B B B B B B

B B B B B B B

Trace the lowercase letters.

b b b b b b b

b b b b b b b

Circle the letter B & b

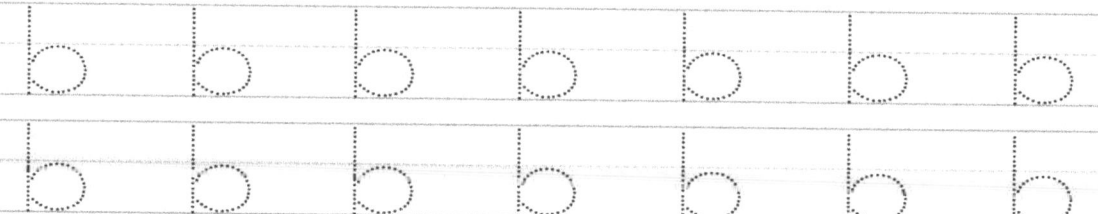

Bee

1

2

3

4

5

 Your Turn:

Crunched it.

Mmmm... that cone was TOO good.

Trace the uppercase letters.

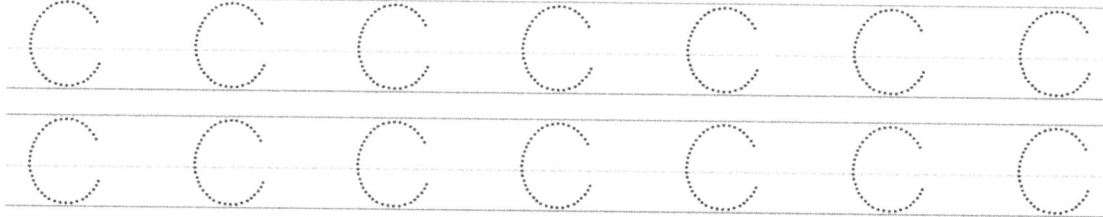

Trace the lowercase letters.

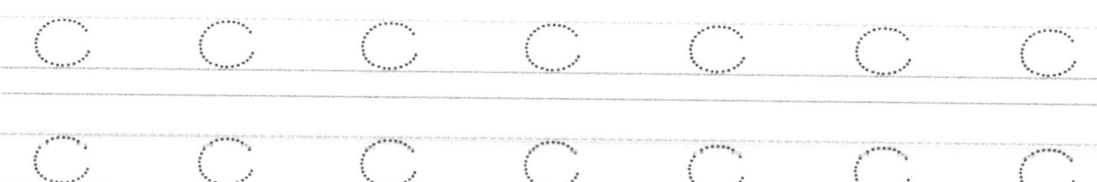

Circle the letter C & c

C W c k J e d A g
d t a R L C m b z x
w b E e g s z K J c N

Cat

1

2

3

4

5

 **Your Turn:**

draw, trace, and color!

 Decorated It

Sprinkles, gummies,
marshmallows—
OH MY!

Trace the uppercase letters.

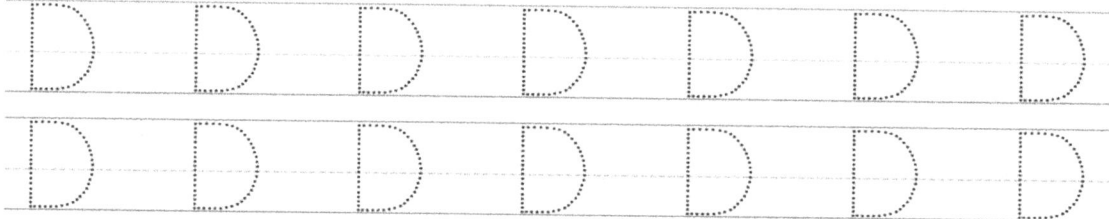

Trace the lowercase letters.

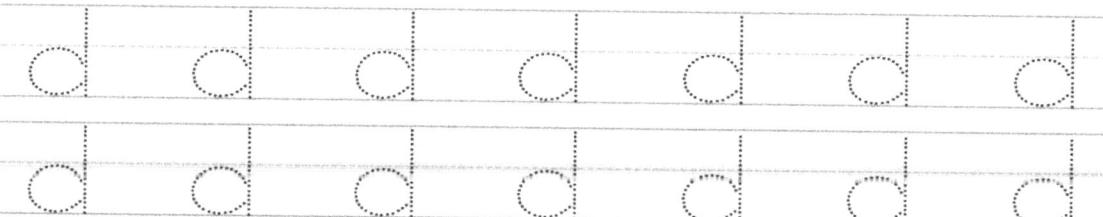

Circle the letter D & d

C W c k J e d r z g
d t a D L C m b x
w D E e g s z D J c N

Dog

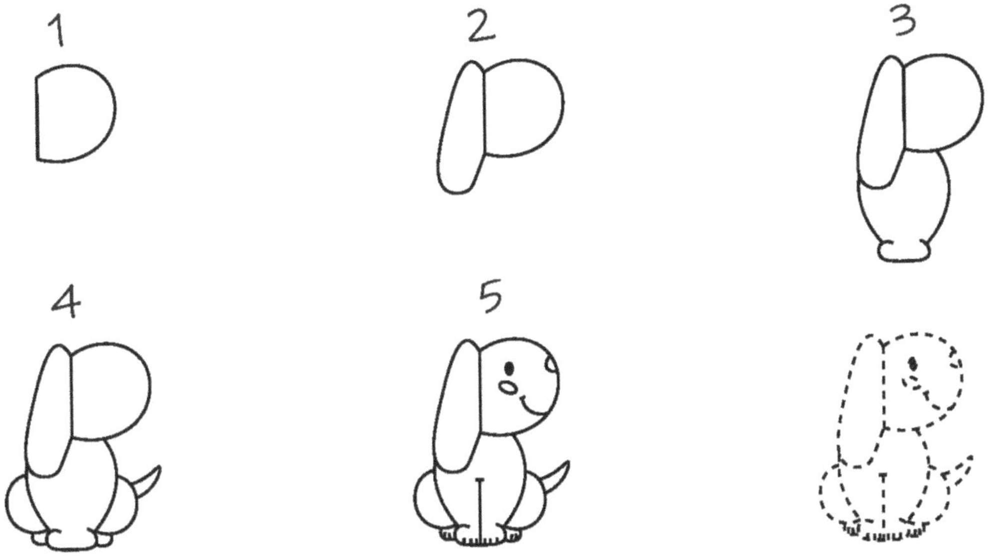

1

2

3

4

5

Your Turn:

draw, trace, and color!

Examined it

E had a checklist: 10 scoops, 2 cherries, 1 banana.

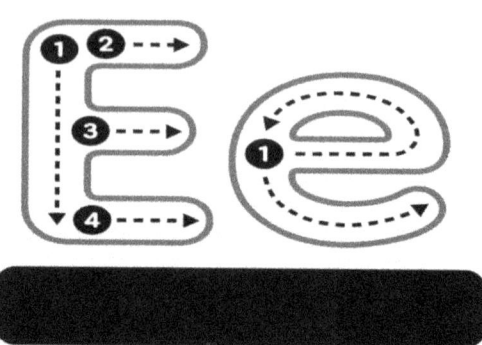

Trace the uppercase letters.

E E E E E E E

F F F F F F F

Trace the lowercase letters.

e e e e e e e

e e e e e e e

Circle the letter E & e

E W e k J e d r z g
d t a D L C m b x
W D E e g s z E J c N

Elephant

1

E

2

3

4

5

 **Your Turn:**

draw, trace, and color!

Flipped it!

Uh oh! Upside down
ice cream
everywhere!

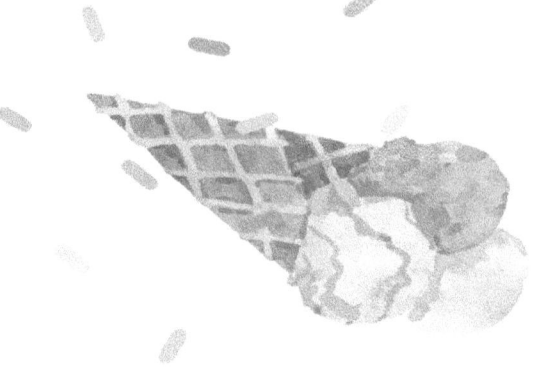

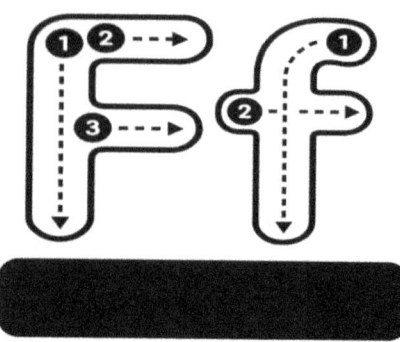

Trace the uppercase letters.

F F F F F F

F F F F F F

Trace the lowercase letters.

f f f f f f f

f f f f f f f

Circle the letter F & f.

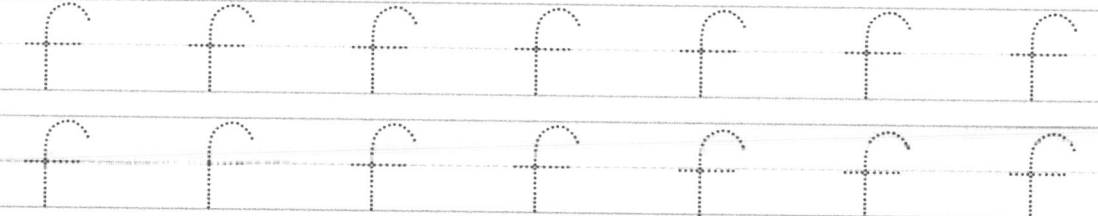

B W P K F e d A z g
d t a R L O m f x
c F E e g s z K j a N

Fish

1

2

3

4

5

 Your Turn:

draw, trace, and color!

Gobbled it.!

Big bite, bigger bite...

Can you gobble like G?

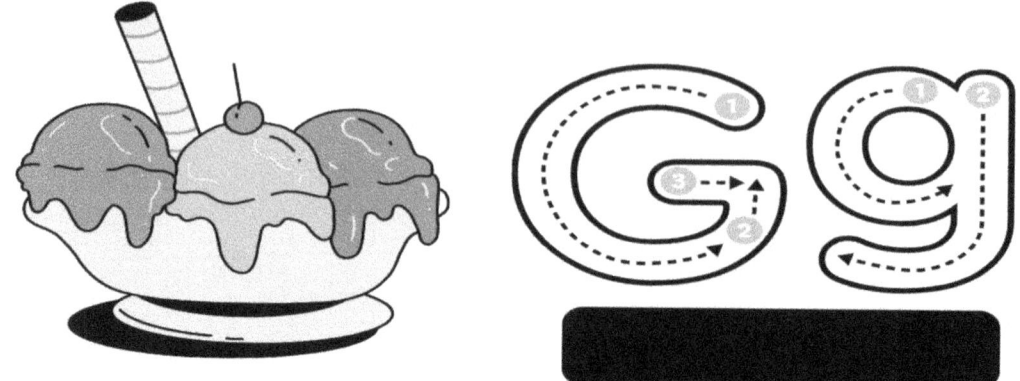

Trace the uppercase letters.

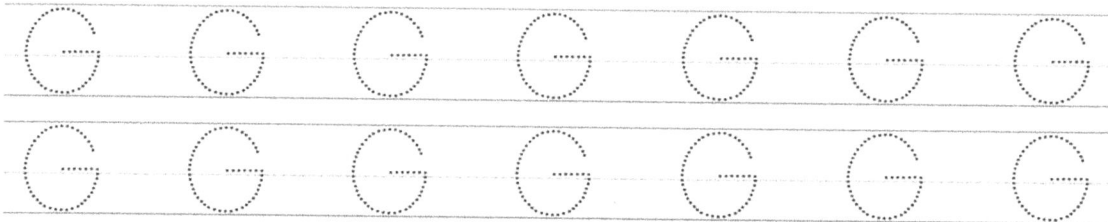

Trace the lowercase letters.

Circle the letter G & g.

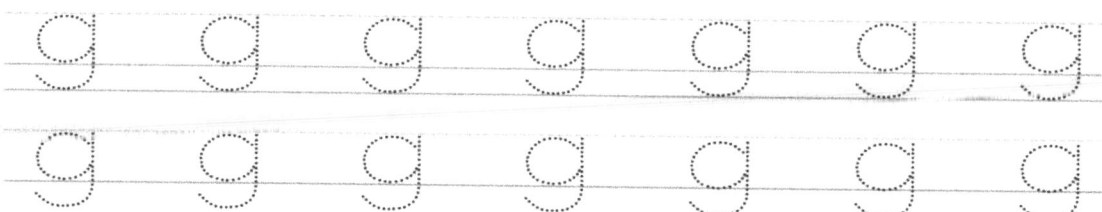

Giraffe

1   2   3

4   5

 <u>Your Turn:</u>

draw, trace, and color!

 Hid it.

In a box? Behind the fridge? Where would YOU hide ice cream?

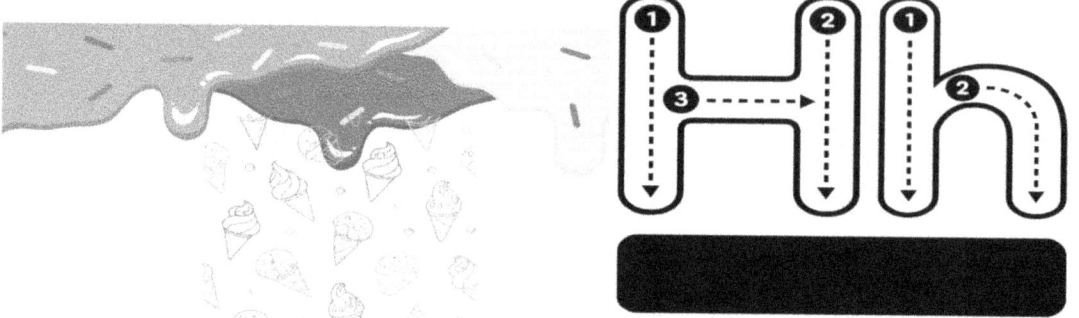

Trace the uppercase letters.

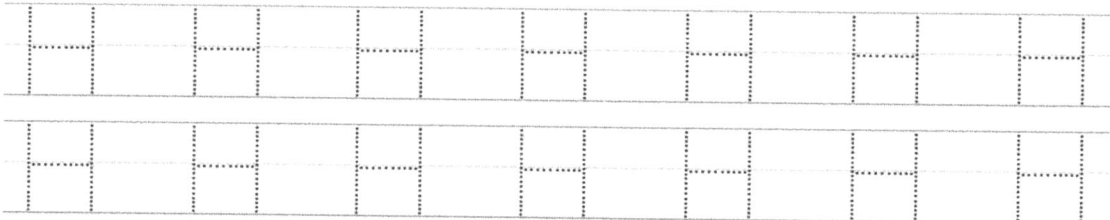

Trace the lowercase letters.

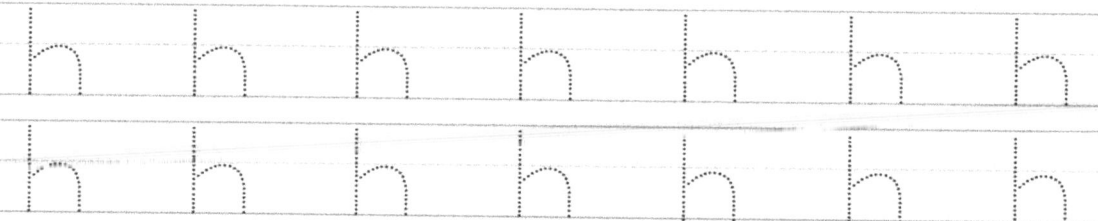

Circle the letter H & h.

H W c k J h d A g
d t a R L H m b z x
w b E g h s z K J c N

Hippo

1

2

3

4

5

Your Turn:

draw, trace, and color!

Iced it

With glittery
frosting and sugar
snowflakes!

Trace the uppercase letters.

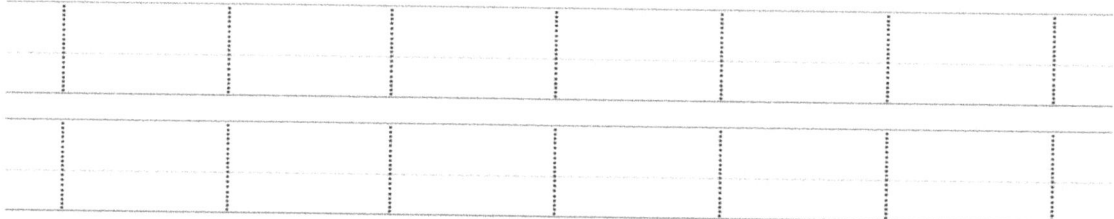

Trace the lowercase letters.

Circle the letter I & i.

I W P K J e d A z i
d t a I L O m u x
c A E e g s i K J a N

Ibis

1

2

3

4

5

Your Turn:

draw, trace, and color!

Juggled it

Three cones in the
air!
Can "J" catch them
all?

Trace the uppercase letters.

J J J J J J J

J J J J J J J

Trace the lowercase letters.

j j j j j j j

j j j j j j j

Circle the letter J & j.

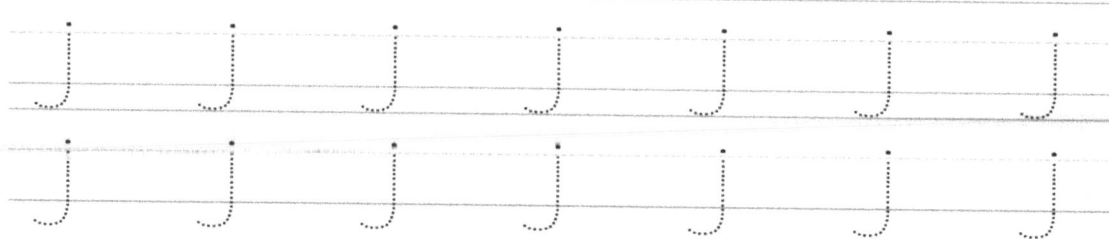

J W P k J e d J z g
d t j R L O m u x
c j E e g s z K J j N

Jellyfish

1

2

3

4

5

Your Turn:

draw, trace, and color!

 Kicked it.

...and SPLAT! The cone took flight.

Trace the uppercase letters.

K K K K K K K

K K K K K K K

Trace the lowercase letters.

k k k k k k k

k k k k k k k

Circle the letter K & k.

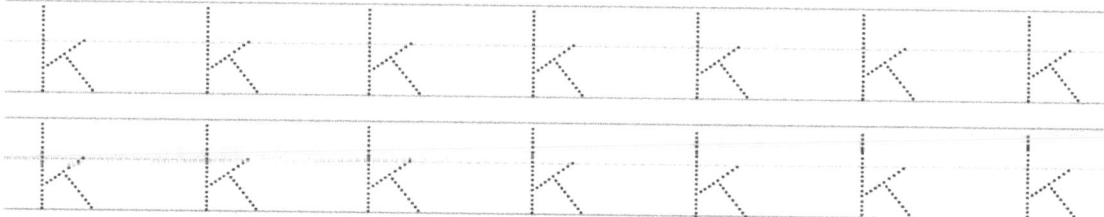

Koala

1

2
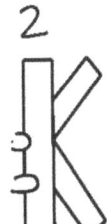

3
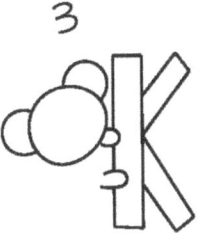

4

5

 <u>Your Turn:</u>

draw, trace, and color!

Licked it

Careful, it's melting!
How many licks
would it take to
finish your cone?

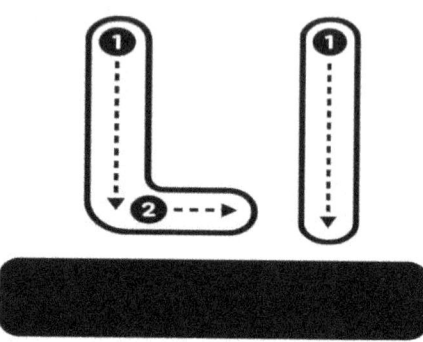

Trace the uppercase letters.

Trace the lowercase letters.

Circle the letter K & k.

K W l k J K d A z g
d k a R L O m L x
l A E e g s z K J a N

Lion

1

2

3

4

5

 Your Turn:

draw, trace, and color!

12

Mmixed it.

Vanilla + chocolate + strawberry = swirl surprise!

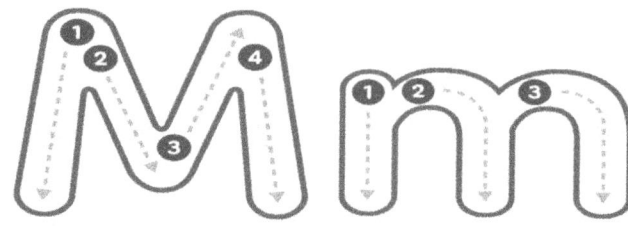

Trace the uppercase letters.

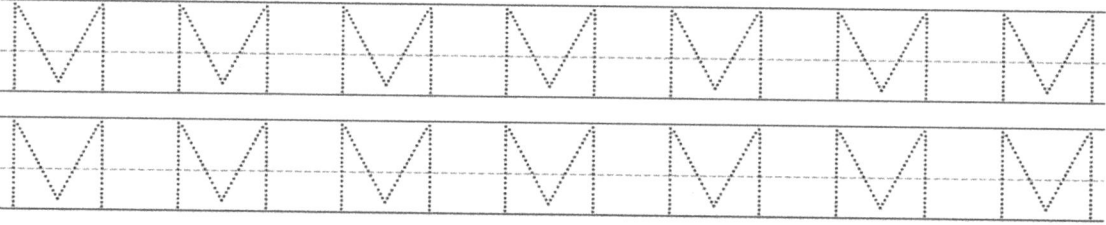

Trace the lowercase letters.

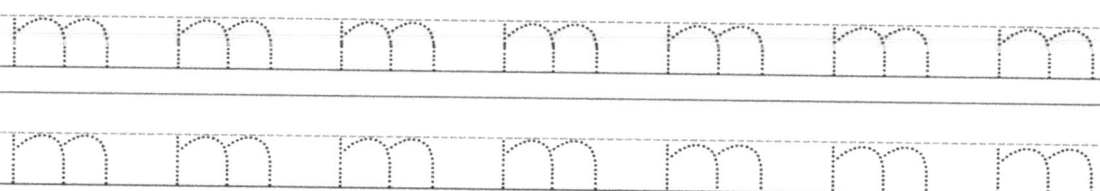

Trace the uppercase & lowercase letters.

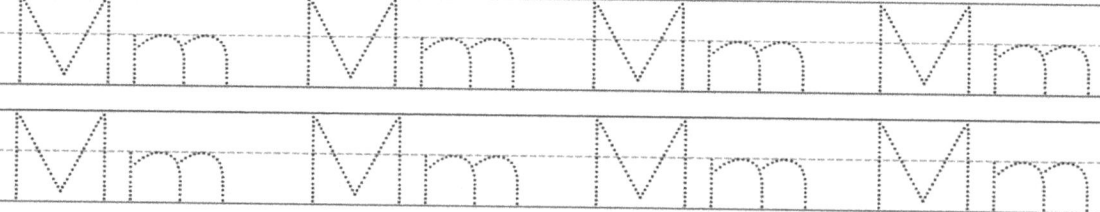

Monkey

1

2

3

4

5

Your Turn:

draw, trace, and color!

 nibbled it..

Tiny bites... someone
is sneaky!

Trace the uppercase letters.

N N N N N N N

N N N N N N N

Trace the lowercase letters.

n n n n n n n

n n n n n n n

Circle the letter N & n.

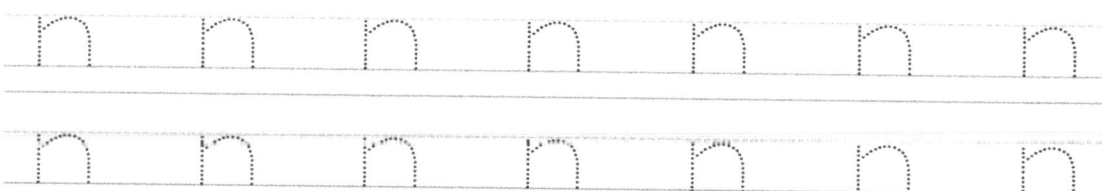

K W P K J K d A z g
n k a R L N m u x
c A E n g s z K j a N

Newt

1

2

3

4

5

Your Turn:

draw, trace, and color!

 offered it.

O is nice. Or is it a trick?
Would YOU share
your ice cream?

Ice Cream

Trace the uppercase letters.

Trace the lowercase letters.

Circle the letter O & o.

Octopus

1

2

3

4

5

 <u>Your Turn:</u>

draw, trace, and color!

P painted it.

Rainbow colors and
polka dots!
Decorate your cone
with art!

Trace the uppercase letters.

P P P P P P P

P P P P P P P

Trace the lowercase letters.

p p p p p p p

p p p p p p p

Circle the letter P & p.

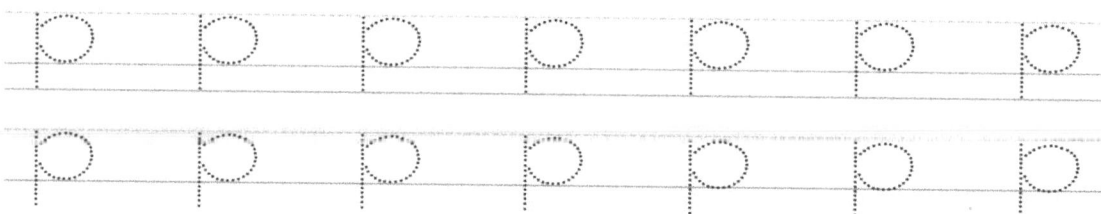

Penguin

1

2

3

4

5

 Your Turn:

draw, trace, and color!

Q questioned it.

"Who took the scoop?" Q asked everyone

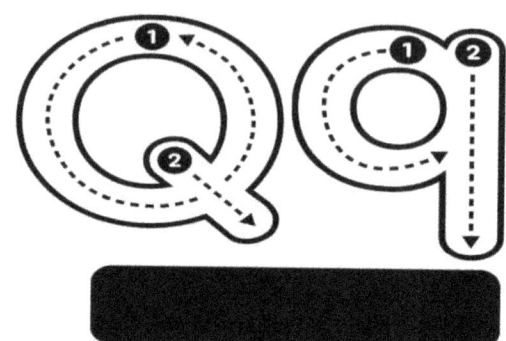

Trace the uppercase letters.

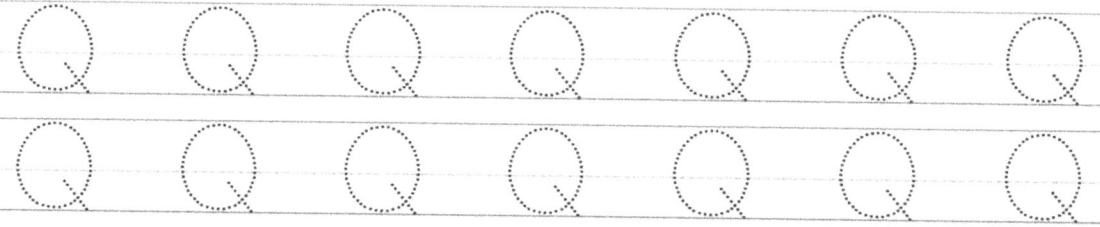

Trace the lowercase letters.

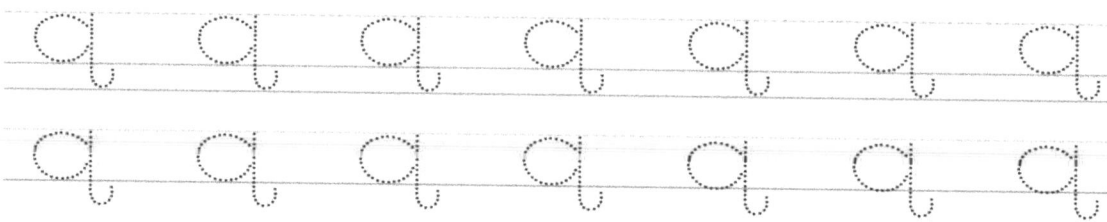

Circle the letter Q & q.

O W P k o k d Q z g
Q K k a R q N m o x
q A E o g s z K J a N

Quail

1
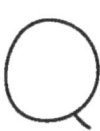

2

3

4

5

 **Your Turn:**

draw, trace, and color!

 raced with it.

Ice cream + running = SPLASH!

Trace the uppercase letters.

R R R R R R R

R R R R R R R

Trace the lowercase letters.

r r r r r r r

r r r r r r r

Circle the letter R & r.

K W P K J K d R z g

R k a R L O m u x

c A E r g s z R J a N

Rabbit

1

2

3

4

5

 Your Turn:

draw, trace, and color!

 Sat on it.

Oh no! Sticky mess!
What sound do you
think that made?

Trace the uppercase letters.

S S S S S S S

S S S S S S S

Trace the lowercase letters.

s s s s s s s

s s s s s s s

Circle the letter S & s.

S W P K S K d s z g
R k a R L O m u x
c A E r g s z R ɔ a N

Snake

1

2

3

4

5

 **Your Turn:**

draw, trace, and color!

Traded it.

One scoop for a toy.
Do you think this is
a fair deal?

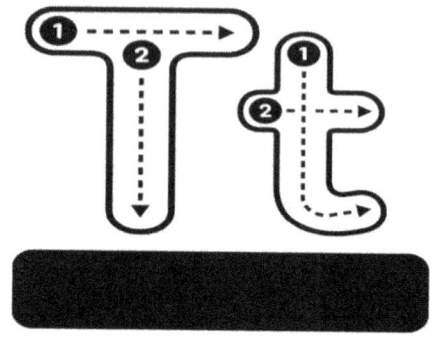

Trace the uppercase letters.

Trace the lowercase letters.

Circle the letter T & t.

S T p K S K d s z g
R k t R L O m u t
c A E r g s z T J a N

Turtle

1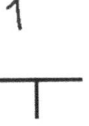

2

3

4

5

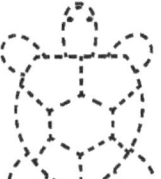

 **Your Turn:**

 draw, trace, and color!

Uncovered
it.

It was hiding under
a napkin!

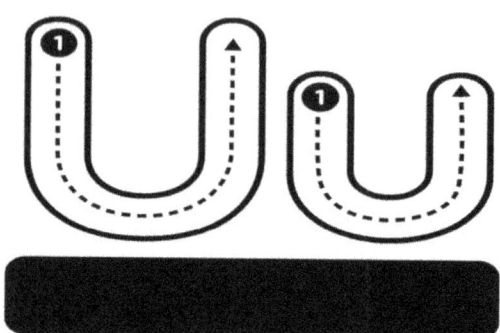

Trace the uppercase letters.

Trace the lowercase letters.

Circle the letter U & u.

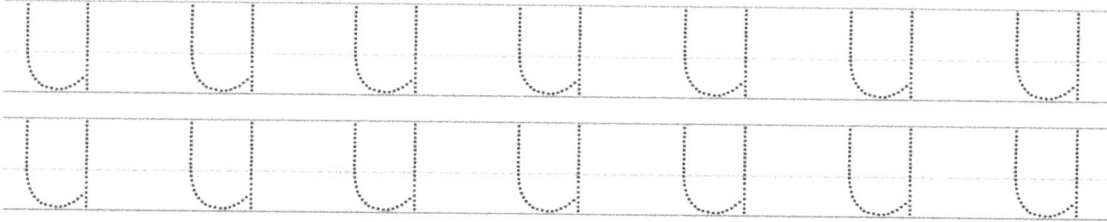

K W P K U K d A z g
u k a R L O m u x
c A U e g s z K j a N

Umbrella

1

2

3

4

5

 <u>Your Turn:</u>

draw, trace, and color!

V vanished with it.

Poof! Cone and all—
gone!

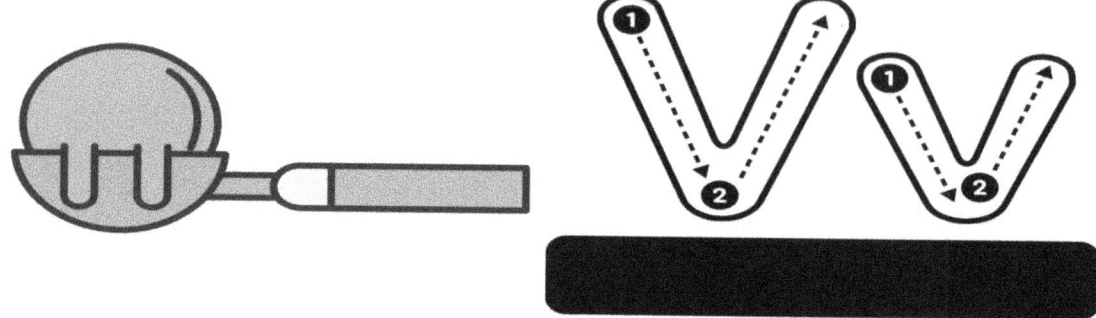

Trace the uppercase letters.

V V V V V V V

V V V V V V V

Trace the lowercase letters.

v v v v v v v

v v v v v v v

Circle the letter V & v.

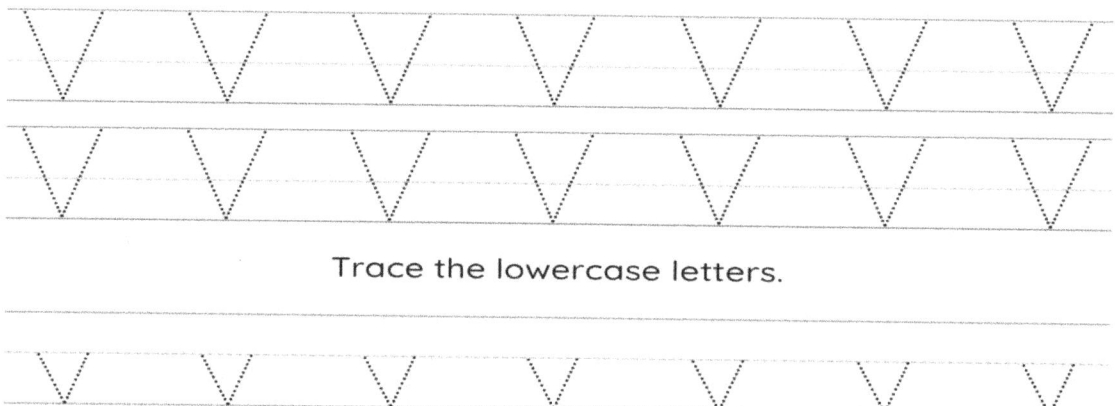

K W P V U K d A z g
V k a R L v m u v
c A U e g s z K j a N

Vulture

1

2

3

4

5

Your Turn:

draw, trace, and color!

W watched it...

he

then tiptoed away
for a sneaky treat!

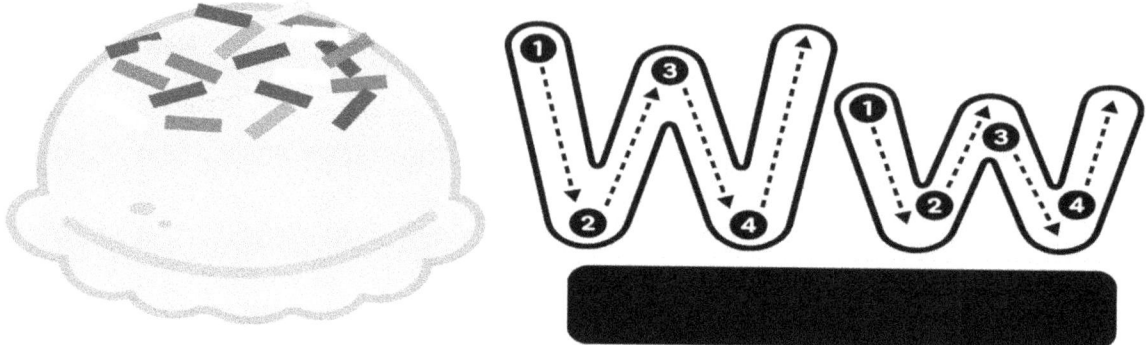

Trace the uppercase letters.

W W W W W W

W W W W W W

Trace the lowercase letters.

w w w w w w

w w w w w w

Circle the letter W & w.

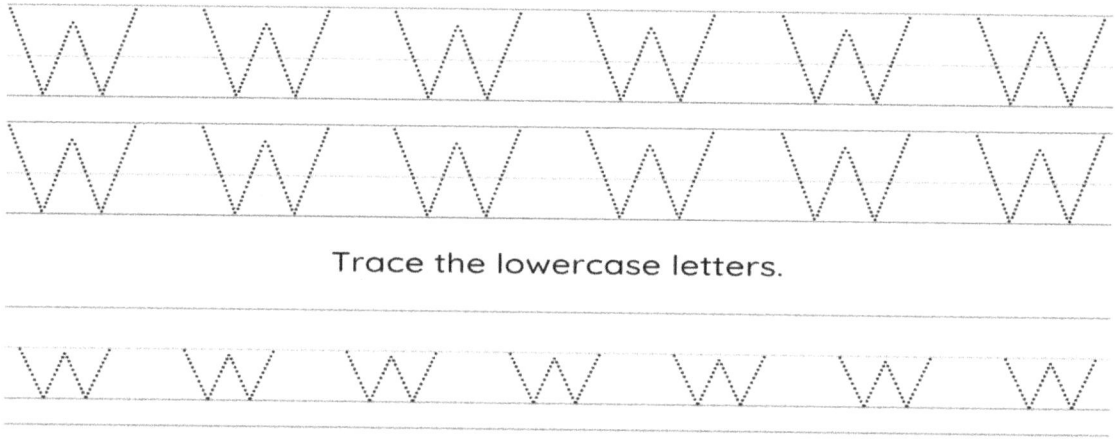

K W P V U K d A g
V k a R w v m W z
c A U e W s z K J a N

Walrus

1

2

3

4

5

 Your Turn:

draw, trace, and color!

X likes X-tra big cones.

Crumbs, drips, and a
cherry stem.
Yummy...

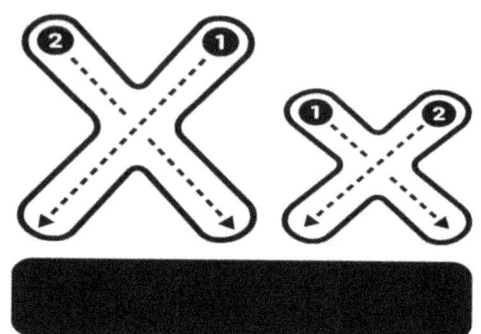

Trace the uppercase letters.

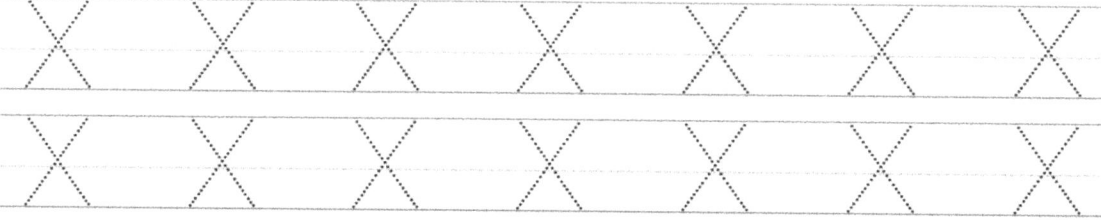

Trace the lowercase letters.

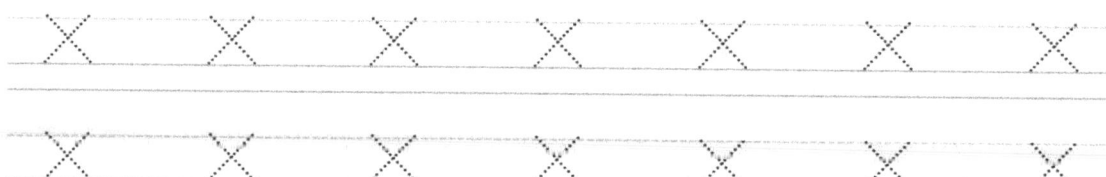

Circle the letter X & x.

S T P K S K x s z g
X X k t R L O m u x
c A E r g s z X J a N

Xylophone

1

2

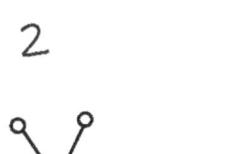

3

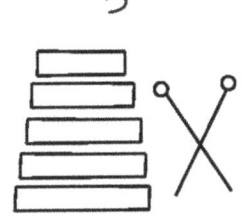

4

5

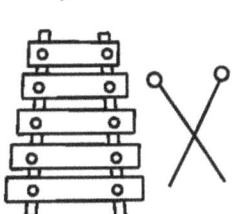

 Your Turn:

draw, trace, and color!

24

 yelled,

"Ice cream is my
favorite dessert"

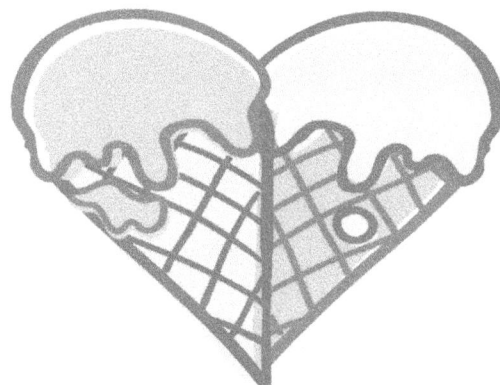

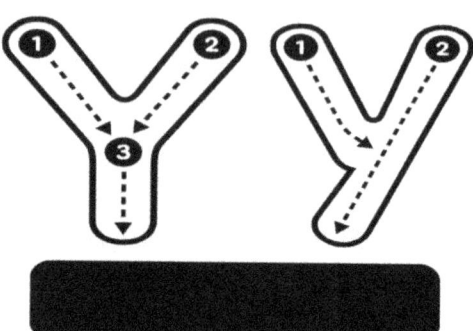

Trace the uppercase letters.

Y   Y   Y   Y   Y   Y   Y

Y   Y   Y   Y   Y   Y   Y

Trace the lowercase letters.

y   y   y   y   y   y   y

y   y   y   y   y   y   y

Circle the letter Y & y.

Y T P K S K d y z g
R k y R L O m u t
c A E r y s z T y a N

Yak

1

Y

2

3

4

5

 <u>Your Turn:</u>

draw, trace,
and color!

25

 **zipped away.**

Wait! Was that a scoop in Z's backpack?!

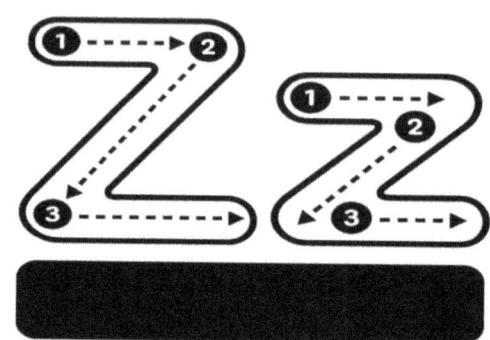

Trace the uppercase letters.

Z Z Z Z Z Z Z

Z Z Z Z Z Z Z

Trace the lowercase letters.

z z z z z z z

z z z z z z z

Circle the letter Z & z.

S T p K S K Z s z g
X k t R L O m u x
c A Z r g z z X J a N

Zebra

1

2

3

4

5

<u>Your Turn:</u>

draw, trace, and color!

We'd Love Your Feedback!

Did your child smile, giggle, or learn something new from our A-Z book?

If this book brought joy or fun learning moments to your home or classroom, we'd be so grateful if you'd leave a short review on Amazon.

Your kind words help other parents, teachers, and kids discover magic inside this book too

www.amazon.com/review/create-review?&asin=BOFD8P6LWH

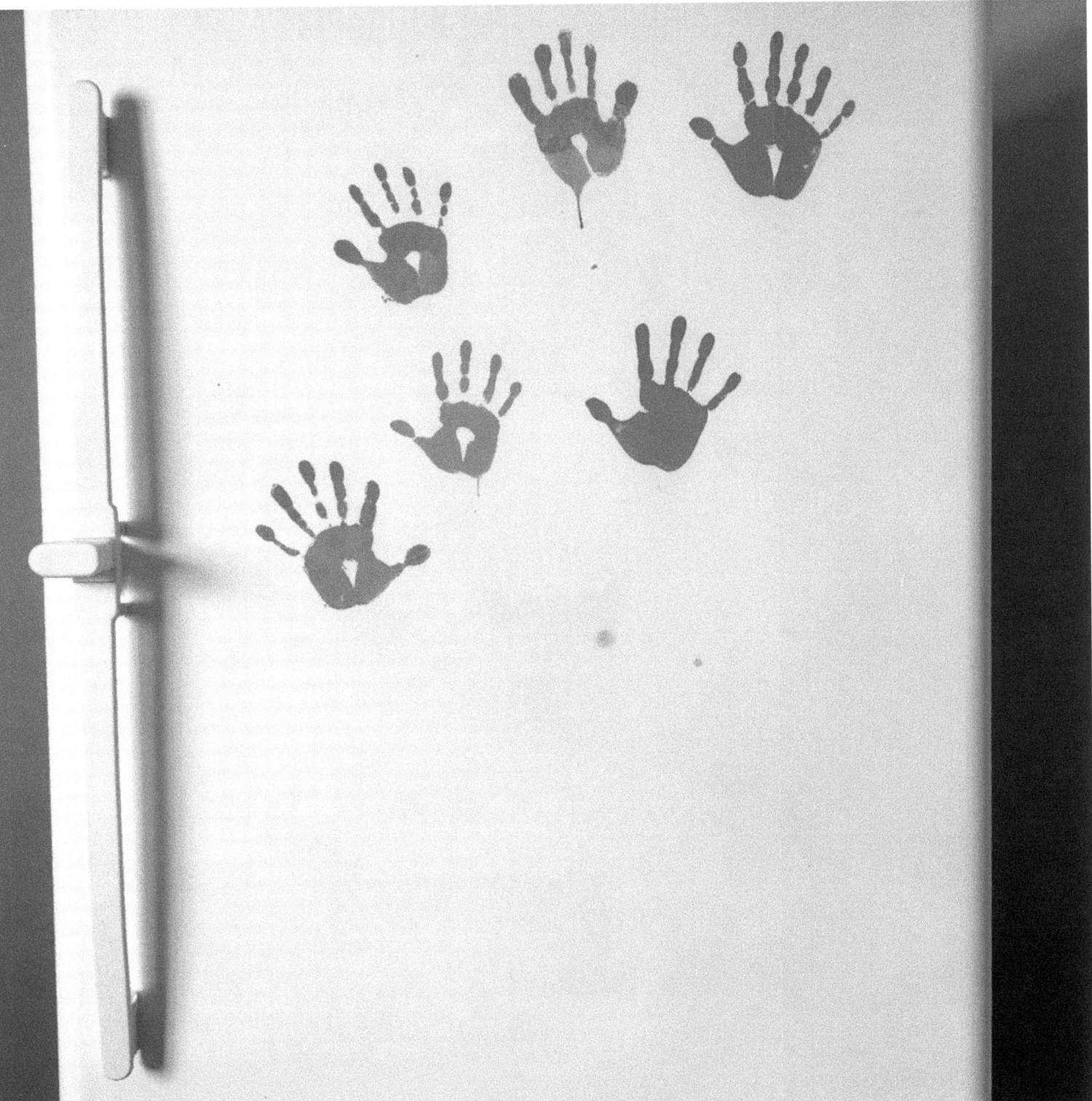